Dragon Music

Jim Fairhall

Acknowledgments:
Some of these poems appeared, in earlier versions, in the following periodicals: *Alligator Juniper, The Butterfly Chronicles, Clackamas Literary Review, Half Tones to Jubilee, Kimera, The Louisville Review, Nimrod, Poetry Now,* and *River King.*

*For Elaine V. Siegel
and the persons who inspired these poems.*

Many thanks to Sandra McPherson, Maria Melendez and Lisa Gonzales for their invaluable editing and other help.

Swan Scythe Press

Department of English
University of California, Davis
One Shields Avenue
Davis, CA 95616

Editor: Sandra McPherson
Associate Editors: Maria Melendez, Lisa Gonzales
Book Design: Maria Melendez

Dragon Music / Jim Fairhall
ISBN 1-930454-04-X

© 2000 by Jim Fairhall

All rights reserved. This book or parts thereof, including artwork, may not be reproduced in any form or by any means, electronic or mechanical, including photocopying, recording, or any information or storage retrieval system now known or to be invented, without written permission from the author, with the exception of brief quotations embodied in critical articles or reviews.

Contents

I

Oracle	7
Mitch	8
Blue Mountain 719	11
Lan	14
Exile	17
The Dirtiest Secret	19

II

Dragon Rising	23
At the Water Puppet Theater	25
Huế Blues	26
Eagle Beach	29
At the Deaf-Mute Café	32
Marble Mountain	35
Minh Mang	36
Notes	39

A great plume of smoke swirls a hundred men high, writhing as a dragon in flight...

—Cao Bá Quát, "The Fire-Boat of the Red-Haired Strangers," c. 1850

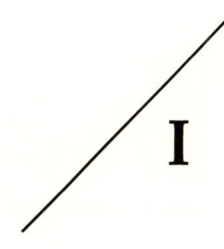

Blue Mountain 719

The South China Sea—
tired, glassy, gun-metal gray—
lobs listless breakers
onto the monsoon-battered beach.
Debris of six months'
stormy tides lies piled on the shore,
and where the sea
has smashed the tennis court,
gray asphalt jags
point skyward recklessly.

I watch my girlfriend, Lan,
drape water-dark fatigues
on the ribs
of rusty concertina wire
(a sea monster's bones)
that spiral darkly down the beach,
as if to shield us
from a Việt Công flotilla,
or maybe to draft sand and surf
on our side, unshifting.

Lan finds the wire,
like the war, unremarkable;
it's there,
useful for hanging laundry.
She wears a gold cross on a chain,
and lives just up the island
in a village, Thuận An—
all refugees from Huế.
The VC swept through like a tide,
foaming her father off with them.

She stretches out the last wet clothes.
A buzzing makes us scan the sky.
Between the slate cloud cover
and the land a tiny plane,

silver-skinned,
flies northward up the coast,
trailing behind it—
amazing thing—
a flutter of snow,
or small white birds, gently falling.

It bumblebees above our heads,
so close we see the pilot,
and then is gone,
a disappearing dot.
The torn air mends,
and simple sounds
flow back: the sea,
still breaking lazily,
and the scuffle
of our flip-flops on the sand.

I pick one of the thin white papers up—
it's folded twice,
and in defiles across each page
march ranks of fuzzy odd
black characters and signs,
and squads of urgent numbers.
——Đây là cái gì? I ask,
hoping she won't crack up
because I've mangled, once again,
her language's soft-toned music.

She likes to read—
especially romantic novels,
with the ivory coarse-cut pages
of old French paperbacks—
but this bores her.
It's just some Army talk, she says;
a victory in Laos:
so many enemies destroyed,

so many blown-up tanks and guns,
so many this...so many that.

We stroll back and latch the hootch's door,
and in the musty dimness
kiss, caress, thud lightly on the floor,
hearing only the tide, booming,
barely aware of what's to come
except her girlfriend,
advancing on us with basket and iron.
Lost in that sweet blind rhythm,
I only want to loiter in her arms,
escaped, ecstatic, islanded.

We rock there on my Army blanket,
a crumpled leaflet
pressed beneath;
we cannot hear the rotors' beat,
nor see the silhouettes
of soldiers swaying from skids,
fleeing Blue Mountain,
weakening and falling.
We only know the slow, sweet rise and fall
of our two bodies and, far off, the sea.

*L*an

1

Morning:
a sunk pale monsoon sky,
with the pine trees
and the gutterless roof edges dripping—
drip-drip, drip, drip-drip—
and the sea, unseen,
muttering.

    ——Where you go, GI?
    ——PX.
    ——You buy me two cig'rette?
    ——What kind?
    ——Selm.

A sparrow-sized brown bird
darts and fusses,
spattering drops
from the branch above us.
What is it called, I wonder,
in Vietnamese?
(Later she says: *con chim*.)

2

On the wet, pine-needle-strewn boardwalk,
on another misty day,
the sight of her makes me shy.
She is a strange, shy bird herself:
her brown eyes jump;
her fingers flutter,
plucking her purple pajama top.

    ——How ol' you?
    ——Twenty-three.

Blue Mountain 719

The South China Sea—
tired, glassy, gun-metal gray—
lobs listless breakers
onto the monsoon-battered beach.
Debris of six months'
stormy tides lies piled on the shore,
and where the sea
has smashed the tennis court,
gray asphalt jags
point skyward recklessly.

I watch my girlfriend, Lan,
drape water-dark fatigues
on the ribs
of rusty concertina wire
(a sea monster's bones)
that spiral darkly down the beach,
as if to shield us
from a Việt Cộng flotilla,
or maybe to draft sand and surf
on our side, unshifting.

Lan finds the wire,
like the war, unremarkable;
it's there,
useful for hanging laundry.
She wears a gold cross on a chain,
and lives just up the island
in a village, Thuận An—
all refugees from Huế.
The VC swept through like a tide,
foaming her father off with them.

She stretches out the last wet clothes.
A buzzing makes us scan the sky.
Between the slate cloud cover
and the land a tiny plane,

silver-skinned,
flies northward up the coast,
trailing behind it—
amazing thing—
a flutter of snow,
or small white birds, gently falling.

It bumblebees above our heads,
so close we see the pilot,
and then is gone,
a disappearing dot.
The torn air mends,
and simple sounds
flow back: the sea,
still breaking lazily,
and the scuffle
of our flip-flops on the sand.

I pick one of the thin white papers up—
it's folded twice,
and in defiles across each page
march ranks of fuzzy odd
black characters and signs,
and squads of urgent numbers.
——*Đây là cái gì?* I ask,
hoping she won't crack up
because I've mangled, once again,
her language's soft-toned music.

She likes to read—
especially romantic novels,
with the ivory coarse-cut pages
of old French paperbacks—
but this bores her.
It's just some Army talk, she says;
a victory in Laos:
so many enemies destroyed,

so many blown-up tanks and guns,
so many this...so many that.

We stroll back and latch the hootch's door,
and in the musty dimness
kiss, caress, thud lightly on the floor,
hearing only the tide, booming,
barely aware of what's to come
except her girlfriend,
advancing on us with basket and iron.
Lost in that sweet blind rhythm,
I only want to loiter in her arms,
escaped, ecstatic, islanded.

We rock there on my Army blanket,
a crumpled leaflet
pressed beneath;
we cannot hear the rotors' beat,
nor see the silhouettes
of soldiers swaying from skids,
fleeing Blue Mountain,
weakening and falling.
We only know the slow, sweet rise and fall
of our two bodies and, far off, the sea.

*L*an

1

Morning:
a sunk pale monsoon sky,
with the pine trees
and the gutterless roof edges dripping —
drip-drip, drip, drip-drip —
and the sea, unseen,
muttering.

>   ——Where you go, GI?
>   ——PX.
>   ——You buy me two cig'rette?
>   ——What kind?
>   ——Selm.

A sparrow-sized brown bird
darts and fusses,
spattering drops
from the branch above us.
What is it called, I wonder,
in Vietnamese?
(Later she says: *con chim*.)

2

On the wet, pine-needle-strewn boardwalk,
on another misty day,
the sight of her makes me shy.
She is a strange, shy bird herself:
her brown eyes jump;
her fingers flutter,
plucking her purple pajama top.

>   ——How ol' you?
>   ——Twenty-three.

——You mar-ry?
——No.
——You have girlfrien'?
——No, frowning mock rue.

She laughs.
A wizened woman with black teeth
speaks to her from behind.
She smiles,
embarrassedly,
and squats to the knot of clothes
heaped dark beside the shower drain.

   3

A soldier wakes me on my cot.
Through the screen door I see,
out in the gauzy midday gray,
a small pajama'd being,
intense.
I tug my boots on guiltily:
Idiot!

——Why you no come?
——Sorry, I—
——You say twel', jabbing her watch.
——I got back la—
——You come.

The women she does laundry with
scrub lunch pots noisily.
She smiles now.
That woman with black teeth—
her grandmother—
grins at me cheerily.
Tomorrow, I say, twelve noon.

4

Whose life is this?
Some legionnaire's, Roman or French?
Hearts move; armies do, too.
Afraid of used words, I cling to facts:
her slim deft honey arms;
that big American iron;
sand, sea, shade and sun, us.

   ——When you go home?
   ——Two months.
   ——You come back?
   ——I'll do my best.
   ——What you say?
   ——Yes...yes.

What if the Gulf of Tonkin
hadn't happened?
What if above the maundering sea
I hadn't heard her voice?
Go figure. Love or war:
where two dark roads converge,
a jolt a shudder.

Exile

Back from red dust for one dazed week,
I wander lost,
my family, my girlfriend ocean-far;
while everywhere
a bright narcotic haze,
more potent than Jamaica Red
or any dope we toked back there,
hangs dazzling on the land,
the people.

I zoom the Thruway up to Albany
(something about college—
as if I have a future here),
marveling at the giant lanes,
the clipped clean median,
the drive of these people
to build boundaries—
stockaded Puritans,
keeping at bay the foreign woods.

It's all a movie.
Watching, I am unheard, invisible, unreal.
No gore, no shock, no talk of war—
just flickers on the bright small screen at supper,
or blurred black print in commuters' tunnel-visions,
which they flip through thinking of money
as the train rams fast through Harlem—
always the waste, unseen,
the ashpits and the dream.

I don't feel safe here: my only haven, trees.
I lurk beneath the fresh green leaves,
hidden in my cammies,
my sandals and black pajamas,
watching,
shouldering my RPG,
aiming at the enemy,

ready to blast that screen
that haze
that blue-glaze, drug abstraction from their eyes.

Then, maybe, I'll think about coming home.
Maybe…

The Dirtiest Secret

The dirtiest secret?
Well, let me tell you this.
There were odd moments when amazement
knocked me dead: not *dead,* but so alive,
that *I* and *me* just guttered out, were lost.
Once I heard water music.
Half in a stream half out—
just after shots had slung me sprawling there—
I listened,
listened to that gurgling glissando,
as if the noisy world had disappeared.
Another time, near Huế,
I saw a gorgeous bus.
On its red flanks
a yellow dragon snaked.
Inside its abdomen, like eggs,
were crammed the white-gowned mourners.

Those moments I would not give back;
nor others.
One midnight in the jungle—
down through dark ghosts of trees,
a pearly film of moonlight dribbled—
I whispered on the horn to Flag,
——Uh, we got a negative sit-rep, over,
and jerked out of my trance when Toby,
a stocky tough black kid from Philly
(only out here   could we have been best friends),
said in my ear,
——Hey man, it's good to hear your voice.

Long afterwards—
a guard upon an island,
I felt as neutral as the sea,
as empty as a bleached shell on the sand—
a girl I'd flirted with

came running because I had stood her up;
her knuckles drummed a tune on me.
She beat me into love that day;
and though the war coughed on,
I've never since remembered it
without that rhythm,
angry-loving, hard-soft   harsh-sweet.

Phan Thị Lan, in the "laundry hootch" at Eagle Beach, near Huế, Việt Nam, March 1971.

Dragon Rising

Hà Nội

Rising toward the rooftree,
its limestone tail
to the cool gray city,
scaled, hissing,
it beckons—my sibyl-guide—
as I spoon my green-flecked soup.

Jump-cut: twenty-six Tếts ago…
Now, my mission solo—
no *Grande Armée*—
I breakfast with the enemy:
a mist of motion far below,
that girl in the kitchen, singing.

Like rappelling from a chopper
(——*Airborne! All the way, sir!*)—
boots shoving off the skid,
plummeting—
I plunge from my hotel, the Rising Dragon,
into the spate

of snorts and roars and jingle-beeps,
of shoulder-pole shuffling women,
of spicy smoke and dust-green leaves,
of glances and cries…mysterious,
like signs
on the mustard walls of old French villas;

then lost, I am washed into the 36 Streets—
this one gourd-brown baskets,
another silver pots,
and that one VCR-TVs,
their sleek black stacks
like booby traps released by time;

at last (survivor's luck)
I shoot the rapids of a silk-store street,

debouching
into the Lake of the Restored Sword,
where on a bench
I beach my ruck,

my own and my country's history,
and listen,
smell,
watch
(I am *here*. It is *now*.)
until small children capture me.

They sell,
from shoulder-hung displays,
new maps of a land I hardly know,
small yellow glossaries
and two white, pregnant books:
Bảo Ninh, *The Sorrow of War*,

and whirling me back,
Graham Greene, *The Quiet American*,
its creased, cheap 1950s look
suggesting an old yearbook.
See! Blind, dumb, that was *you* then —
and there, before you, the dragon.

At the Water Puppet Theater

To up-and-down excited notes
the yellow dragon,
ruby-eyed,
swims, swoops,
dancing like a dragonfly,
like the Venetian-blue acrobat
I tracked, mesmerized,
after the ambush.
I had never seen anything
so beautiful.

In the gurgling quiet
we booby-trapped him,
slim, stripped,
his brown eyes reflecting the tree-webbed sky.
We stalked the stream that night,
dragons awaiting dragons,
until out of blackness
light—
a dragon's eye—
flared once, flared twice...

But now this dragon,
proud-maned,
a water mustang,
is gliding back beneath the screen.
He cannot die.
I clap,
nudged by the plump French lady
next to me who's clapping harder,
transported
by such loveliness, such power.

Huế Blues

Looking back,
it's like remembering a woman—
dark-haired and almond-skinned,
young, beautiful and old,
sometimes serene
and sometimes roiled with passion,
which shook you
as a stalk of young green rice
is shaken by the wind,
though what it meant   you never knew.

In the veiled monsoon morning,
we rumbled across the river.
A tank, burnt-out,
slouched in shore grass like a late, charred toad,
while a bridge gulped air at a broken span.
It was Palm Sunday.
In white *aó dài*,
young women walked or pedaled by,
calmly ignoring
our growling mud-streaked passage.

Now silver-streaked,
armed with a cheerful tourist map,
I stroll the riverbank
in search of a street that bevels off Lê Lợi.
Ah, there: a sign, with yet another hero's name.
It starts to rain.
I walk, ignored by all except cyclo drivers,
who cry out like ancient parrots:
——*Hey, rich foreigner, ride with me!*
There are no women in *aó dài*.

Those groaning-geared, packed cattle trucks
were hauling us,
our jungle boots just barely scuffed with red,
to our new companies.

We humped, thumped the green bush,
losing our cherries
and yet far from the hip-sway,
the silken-white glide
of those women of Huế.

No, I just don't know these streets.
I only recollect
our crossing the brown wide river,
the market's sea of bamboo hats,
a faded sign—
Brasseries et glacières d'Indochine—
those taut yet flowing costumes
and the spire and the bulk,
dirty-white, of a cathedral,
and the stiff-stretched arms of a tall pale Christ.

My guidebook says:
Church of the Mother of Perpetual Help.
We *needed* help:
from her, St. Christopher, from *some*body.
One hour after I'd joined my unit,
amid an echoing black cloud,
a kid flew lengthwise in the air;
he rolled, with a jumper's lazy grace,
a woman's height above the ground.
He was, as someone said, experienced.
And *I?*

Not quite so huge as I recall,
the church, hemmed in by lanes,
affords no angle for a photograph.
I point my lens at Christ and shoot.
Amid *ha-ha*'s,
fragments of heads and hands explode,
as little kids dance-hop.
——What you do? cries one.
Good question.

Out in that mad, green maze of hills,
the Rocket Belt,
our job was to protect the land below.
The enemy played tag with us.
One midnight on a hill of grass,
mosquito-plagued and restless,
I watched six star-streaks rise,
rise out of the inky jungle
and, like arrows,
arc toward the city's faint far glow.
They were so beautiful,
I hoped there would be more.

———*Hoa Kỳ?*
———*Phải*, I tell the kids:
an American ghost;
a cherry, first day back.
Gray tracers strike the rooftops and the trees.
Warm-spattered, I retreat toward the river;
tired now, tired of tracking,
in overgrown trails of nerves,
vague streets
and—like a green-streaked jungle ruin—
the outlines of a creature
fearsome, lovely   long gone.

Eagle Beach

The low-slung, tire-ringed, tar-smelling ferry,
the jeeps and cargoes,
the GIs and those witch-capped women
balancing chickens, greens, misshapen roots
and mysteries from the market at Huế,
20 klicks and a world down the road—
all seem more real
than this slim new bridge,
onto which, in morning haze,
we pedal our clunky bikes.

The surprising long arch
and wake-scrawled bay behind us,
we plant our feet and breathe salt air,
scanning from village to sea.
Nothing. Nothing familiar.
My 19-year-old Danish friends,
curious, wait.
They know little of history,
less of me and this island:
just that I said, There's a beautiful beach.

Under oyster clouds blowing in fast,
we ride to the toll gate,
lean down the sand-swept lane.
There are no yards with palms and feather pines,
no thatched-roof houses of friendlies.
Low concrete huts,
tea-splotched, crowd the road.
Squads of young men, VC,
keep staring at Viking-blonde Dorte.

At last a dark green grove
and then the sea, in sudsy fury,
raving from the horizon,
charges a stretch of trash-strewn sand.
We halt, breasting the wind.

Anders sports his market find,
a Hô Chí Minh T-shirt, carmine,
which ripples around his sapling torso,
flapping like a flag.

So this is it!
I feel like my dad, having schlepped his kids
to a chilly beach in Normandy,
where he got misty-eyed,
embarrassing us.
Tired, riding to beat the storm,
we duck into the island's lone café.
I sweat, half swooned, over rusty soup.
A faraway boombox,
through the rain, belts Swedish rock.
Rock Around the Clock. Plymouth Rock. Bunk.

A man in Nikes and black jeans skips in,
keen to practice English;
young, until his eyes' blood-flowers loom.
  ——Long time (stained smile)
Americans were here.
I fish my muddy snaps: daguerreotypes
of low wood watchtowers, nicknamed hootches,
a minigolf course in the sand,
like an outpost of some warrior kingdom—
Champa, perhaps, or the Chinese dragon.

For Hòa, it's 25 years ago.
He and his adviser, Captain Anderson,
traded American slang,
brothers,
though afterwards his brother never wrote.
  ——You *Americans...*
Then he brightens,
peers hard at my girlfriend Lan.
Yes, yes, she's familiar;
she had American children.

A woman with plum-dark eyes,
waiting like him for the ODP
(a slower leaving than ours,
like sucking a bittersweet leaf
that never gets softer, sweeter),
agrees. She stares at me,
a stranger's mom herself.
⎯⎯But where did she go? I ask.
On a boat, they say,
maybe Philippines…
maybe she die.

I apologize to my left-out friends.
Dorte demurs: No, no, this is history,
it's the best part of our trip.
Hòa says that he teases his younger son,
brown-haired, calling him: *the American*.
From his loser's ID card,
a bright-eyed lieutenant smiles:
⎯⎯Girls, girls turn and look me then.
The rain quiets. We say goodbye.
We race the clouds across the bay,
big gray puffballs, scudding towards Huế.

At the Deaf-Mute Café

1

We shelter, as if cave-dwellers,
from the splashing, glistening sheet.

Old women stir-fry in the front,
flames leaping by the riptide street.

More backpackers, sopped, dash in,
babbling in English, French, German,

but know little of what's out there,
beyond what five senses soak in.

A boy who's selling nylon capes—
Goofy Grape—grins, proffers, gestures.

No takers. Coolly, like Harpo,
he rests his calf on a girl's

thigh. She brushes him off, giggling.
At the guys he throws shadow slaps,

gabbling, smiling, then runs to meet
more streaming, blinking, flame-lit shapes.

2

The cloud-hid moon has spun three days,
rebirthing the Year of the Rat.

Hô Chí Minh grins from Anders' chest,
barring me from young cheerful chat.

They ask, Did you find your girlfriend?
Should I say, On the back of Hòa's

motorbike, I slithered through rain
and ate pork rice at every house,

pleased feasters staring at pictures
of ghosts—all of us, them and ghosts,

a stone's throw from the tossed gray bay
where, from the sea, French fireboats

steamed, then snaked upriver and shelled
the dragon-shocked court at Huế,

whose upstart dynasty's sovereign
saw, through smoke, the moon spin crazily?

3

Or did I fable this, the past,
my own and firestorm-haunted Huế's?

Hòa said, when too soon I slid back
white fat, You don't really know us.

And they know *us*? I thought. A bang
made me jump: a boy with a basin

tromped the lane, calling a meeting.
——In the war, Hòa said, mean VC come.

Our jokey waitress pantomimes.
In a red dress like a majorette's,

she two-steps, spins, looks blank when—dumb—
I speak, and points to her crimson lips.

Like players we gesticulate,
as in a traveling mime show.

The rain abates; street noises rise.
New shadows, flaring, come and go.

A woman with plum-dark eyes,
waiting like him for the ODP
(a slower leaving than ours,
like sucking a bittersweet leaf
that never gets softer, sweeter),
agrees. She stares at me,
a stranger's mom herself.
         ——But where did she go? I ask.
On a boat, they say,
maybe Philippines…
maybe she die.

I apologize to my left-out friends.
Dorte demurs: No, no, this is history,
it's the best part of our trip.
Hòa says that he teases his younger son,
brown-haired, calling him: *the American*.
From his loser's ID card,
a bright-eyed lieutenant smiles:
         ——Girls, girls turn and look me then.
The rain quiets. We say goodbye.
We race the clouds across the bay,
big gray puffballs, scudding towards Huế.

At the Deaf-Mute Café

1

We shelter, as if cave-dwellers,
from the splashing, glistening sheet.

Old women stir-fry in the front,
flames leaping by the riptide street.

More backpackers, sopped, dash in,
babbling in English, French, German,

but know little of what's out there,
beyond what five senses soak in.

A boy who's selling nylon capes—
Goofy Grape—grins, proffers, gestures.

No takers. Coolly, like Harpo,
he rests his calf on a girl's

thigh. She brushes him off, giggling.
At the guys he throws shadow slaps,

gabbling, smiling, then runs to meet
more streaming, blinking, flame-lit shapes.

2

The cloud-hid moon has spun three days,
rebirthing the Year of the Rat.

Hô Chí Minh grins from Anders' chest,
barring me from young cheerful chat.

They ask, Did you find your girlfriend?
Should I say, On the back of Hòa's

motorbike, I slithered through rain
and ate pork rice at every house,

pleased feasters staring at pictures
of ghosts—all of us, them and ghosts,

a stone's throw from the tossed gray bay
where, from the sea, French fireboats

steamed, then snaked upriver and shelled
the dragon-shocked court at Huế,

whose upstart dynasty's sovereign
saw, through smoke, the moon spin crazily?

      3

Or did I fable this, the past,
my own and firestorm-haunted Huế's?

Hòa said, when too soon I slid back
white fat, You don't really know us.

And they know *us*? I thought. A bang
made me jump: a boy with a basin

tromped the lane, calling a meeting.
——In the war, Hòa said, mean VC come.

Our jokey waitress pantomimes.
In a red dress like a majorette's,

she two-steps, spins, looks blank when—dumb—
I speak, and points to her crimson lips.

Like players we gesticulate,
as in a traveling mime show.

The rain abates; street noises rise.
New shadows, flaring, come and go.

A NOTE ON PRONUNCIATION

Vietnamese has six tones (five in the south), as well as diacritical marks, affecting pronunciation and meaning:

Middle strong: (no marker)		ma (ghost)
High rising:	´	má (mother)
Low falling:	`	mà (which)
Middle rising then slightly falling:	ˀ	mả (tomb)
High slightly falling then rising:	~	mã (horse)
Very low:	.	mạ (rice seedling)

NOTES TO THE POEMS

Epigraph
    Cao Bá Quát [kow bá kwót]: Poet-diplomat. After a British steamship passed his junk, he wrote "The Fire-Boat of the Red-Haired Strangers," which ends with a warning to Westerners.

"Oracle"
    Cam Ranh Bay [kom ron]: Site of naval base, troop transfer center, hospital, etc.

"Mitch"
    Beeham: Firebase Birmingham—artillery outpost on a hill above the Perfume River, west of Huế.
    brownbar: Second Lieutenant.
    re-up: At that time infantrymen could get rear jobs by reenlisting for three years.
    Eagle Beach: The in-country R&R center of the 101st Airborne Division; on a barrier island near Huế.

"Blue Mountain 719": Operation *Lam Sản* (Blue Mountain) 719—South Việt Nam's heralded, disastrous invasion of Laos in February 1971. Some soldiers tried to flee by hanging onto the skids of retreating helicopters.
Lan [lon]: Female name meaning "orchid."
Thuận An [tooạn ahn]: Village near Eagle Beach.
Huế [hwáy]: Former imperial city, seized during the Tết offensive.
Đây là cái gì? [day làh kái yè]: What is this?

"Lan"
con chim [kawn chim]: Bird.
Gulf of Tonkin: Night attacks (real and imagined) by patrol boats on an American destroyer in 1964; also the "Tonkin Gulf resolution," freeing LBJ to widen the war.

"Exile"
RPG: Rocket-propelled grenade launched through a tube.

"The Dirtiest Secret"
Flag: Command post of an infantry company's CO, including his radio man.
sit-rep: Situation report.

"Dragon Rising": Original name (*Thăng Long*) of Hà Nội. In legend the Vietnamese are descended from the Dragon Lord of the Lac people.
36 Streets: Oldest quarter of Hà Nội.
Bảo Ninh [bỏw neen]: Novelist and former soldier.

"Huế Blues"
cyclos [seecloze]: Pedicabs.
aó dài [ów yài]: Silk tunic dress with a side slit; worn over silk trousers.
Lê Lợi [leh lọy]: Leader of a revolt (1418-26) ending China's last full occupation.
Hoa Kỳ [hwah keè]: America; American.
Phải [fỷ]: Yes; right.

"Eagle Beach"
> *Champa:* Kingdom once encompassing much of what is now southern Việt Nam.
> *Hòa* [hwàh]: Male name; also a prefix for words meaning "peace," "harmony," etc.
> *ODP:* Orderly Departure Program for Vietnamese who served over three years in prison or suffered other penalties as a result of wartime employment by the U.S.

"At the Deaf-Mute Café"
> *Year of the Rat:* Each Tết, the three-day lunar new year festival, ushers in an animal-named new year.

"Marble Mountain": Hill near Đà Nẵng with shrine and caves.

"Minh Mang" [min mẹng]: Minh Mệnh, emperor from 1820 to 1840.
> *The Guitarist of Long Thành* [lawm tàhn]: In this poem (1813) Nguyễn Du [ngweuhen tzoo] evokes his return to Hà Nội after many years' absence.
> *Citadel:* Built in Huế by the first Nguyễn emperors, Minh Mệnh and his father.
> *camps:* Postwar prisons for South Vietnamese officers and officials.
> *New Life Hamlet:* Rural settlement for political outcasts and their families.

7610